TinkerActive WORKBOOKS

Pre-K · SCIENCE · AGES 4–5

by Megan Hewes Butler

illustrated by Chad Thomas

educational consulting by Randi House

Odd Dot · New York

Living Things

People are **alive**. They need air to breathe and food and water to grow.

Circle the people at the park.

WELCOME TO TINKERTOWN PARK

You're alive, too! Draw a picture of yourself.

Plants and animals are alive, too. They also need air to breathe and food and water to grow.

Color the plants and animals.

Draw a line to lead the guinea pig to its food and water.

Why does this guinea pig need food and water?
Tell a friend or family member!

Not all things are living. A rock is not alive. It does not need air to breathe, or food and water to grow.

Cross out things that are not alive.

Color the things that are alive.

Can you find any of these things when you look out your window? What else do you see outside that's alive?

Look around your home. Draw two things you see that are alive.

My dog Boxer

LET'S START!

GATHER THESE TOOLS AND MATERIALS.

Glass jar with a wide mouth and a screw-on lid

Nail
(with an adult's help)

Hammer
(with an adult's help)

Small rocks

Dirt

Small plant

Small cup of water

Small piece of
fruit or vegetable

Paper bowls or cups

Small cardboard boxes or shoeboxes

Modeling clay
(optional)

LET'S TINKER!

Most living things can move on their own. Can any of your materials move on their own, without anything touching them?

Move your body. Can you use your body to make your materials move? Are any of your materials living things?

LET'S MAKE: BUG HABITAT!

1. With the help of an adult, **add** air to your habitat: **Poke** six or more small holes in the lid of the glass jar with a hammer and nail.

2. **Fill** the bottom of the jar with a layer of small rocks. Then **add** a layer of dirt. Then **add** a small plant in the dirt.

3. Add water to your habitat: **Sprinkle** water on the dirt until it is damp. If the dirt dries out a few days later, **do** this again.

4. Add food to your habitat. **Add** a small piece of a fruit or vegetable, like a piece of an apple or a tiny bit of carrot.

5. Hunt for a mealworm, cricket, beetle, or other bug. **Place** it in your jar and screw the lid on tight.

6. Check the dirt and food a few days later, and if the dirt is dry, add a little more water. Pull out any food that's left and replace it with something fresh. **Watch** your bug move and grow!

LET'S ENGINEER!

Brian loves collecting objects while he hikes. This time, he found rocks, a few twigs, a flower, and a button! He wants to organize his objects into living and nonliving things.

How can Brian sort his objects?

Go on a walk and **collect** some living and nonliving things. Then build something to sort them. **Think** about how you sort other small items—what materials would make a good bin for them? How will someone know where to put a living or nonliving thing? Then **sort** your materials! Do you have any living things? If not, **model** one out of clay.

PROJECT 1: DONE!
Get your sticker!

My Body

You are alive. Your body grows and changes.

Start with the baby and trace the line through the life cycle of a person.

baby

child

teen

adult

Circle the things that you can do now that you couldn't do when you were a baby.

Your body parts help you move.

Draw a line to match each action to the body part that moves. Then do the action with your own body!

mouth

hand

eye

hip

foot

Draw your face. Then draw a line to label each part.

hair   eye   nose   mouth   ear

Your body needs food and water to grow. Say the name of each fruit and vegetable aloud. Color the food items you like to eat.

apple

tomato

grapes

carrot

banana

strawberry

watermelon

You eat, sleep, breathe, and move. Animals do, too. Draw a line to match each person and animal doing the same thing.

LET'S START!

GATHER THESE TOOLS AND MATERIALS.

Crayons

Paper

6 index cards

Paper bag

Paper plate

Small items, like:
string, buttons, twist ties, cotton balls, paper clips

LET'S TINKER!

Trace your hand on a piece of paper. Then **trace** a family member's hand. How are they the same or different? Which is bigger? Why?

LET'S MAKE: GO, GO, GO GAME!

1. With the help of an adult, **write** one action word on the front of each index card: hop, skip, crawl, slide, dance, gallop.

2. Draw one place in your home on the back of each card, like a chair, table, or door.

3. Place the cards in the paper bag.

4. Take turns with a friend or family member to play. To start, **pick** two cards. The first tells you what PLACE to go. The second tells you the ACTION to do! (You may hop to a chair, or dance to a table, etc.)

DANCE

LET'S ENGINEER!

The MotMots made some new friends at school. Dimitri wants to take a picture, but his camera is broken.

How can the MotMots make a picture of their friends instead?

Use your materials to make a picture of your face! **Start** with a paper plate for your head. What can you use to show other body parts, like your eyes, ears, nose, and mouth? What about hair? What other body parts can you show?

PROJECT 2: DONE!
Get your sticker!

Animals

Animals are alive. They grow and change. Baby animals grow up and often look similar to their parents.

Draw a line to match each baby animal to what it will look like when it is fully grown.

Look closely at this baby rattlesnake and baby clown fish. Then draw what you think their parents might look like.

Animals have body parts to help them move, eat, protect themselves, and communicate.

Look at the body parts of an elephant. Point at the parts that you have, and say the names aloud. Then color the parts that you don't have.

ear

eye

trunk

foot

Circle the mouth on each animal. Then make the sound that each animal makes.

Animals live in **habitats** where they can get the food, water, and shelter that they need.

Draw a line to lead each animal to its home in the forest habitat.

There are many different habitats on the Earth for animals to live in. Draw a line to match each animal to its habitat.

whale

rain forest

polar bear

arctic

toucan

grassland

zebra

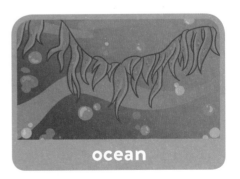

ocean

Take a walk around your habitat at home. Show a friend or family member where you get the food and water that you need!

LET'S START!

Natural materials, like:
leaves, pine needles, sticks, seeds, flowers, bark, grass, rocks

Construction paper

Scissors
(with an adult's help)

Glue stick

Markers

LET'S TINKER!

Look at your materials—which could be found in an animal's habitat? Which would not be? Why? **Sort** the items that could be found in an animal's habitat into a pile. Which kinds of animals might live around materials like these?

LET'S MAKE: SNAKE FAMILY!

1. With the help of an adult, **cut** a sheet of paper into five strips.

2. Bend one strip into a ring and seal it with a glue stick.

3. Bend another strip into a ring that loops through the first ring, and seal it with a glue stick.

4. Continue until all the strips have been used.

5. Use scraps of paper and a marker to add snake eyes and a tongue to your baby snake.

6. Next, **make** a parent snake to go with the baby! How will it be similar or different? How many rings will it use—will it be longer or shorter?

LET'S ENGINEER!

Amelia and Brian found a small round rock that looks like an egg. They are pretending that it might hatch! What pretend animal could be inside?

How can the MotMots make a home for the egg?

Use your natural materials to build a small nest. Which materials could make a soft place for an egg? Which materials could help to hold the nest together?

What would your pretend animal need once it has hatched?

PROJECT 3: DONE!
Get your sticker!

Plants are alive. They grow and change. Trace the numbers 1, 2, 3, and 4 to put the illustrations in order from first to last.

Plants have many parts to help them live and grow. Say the name of each plant part aloud. Then color the plant.

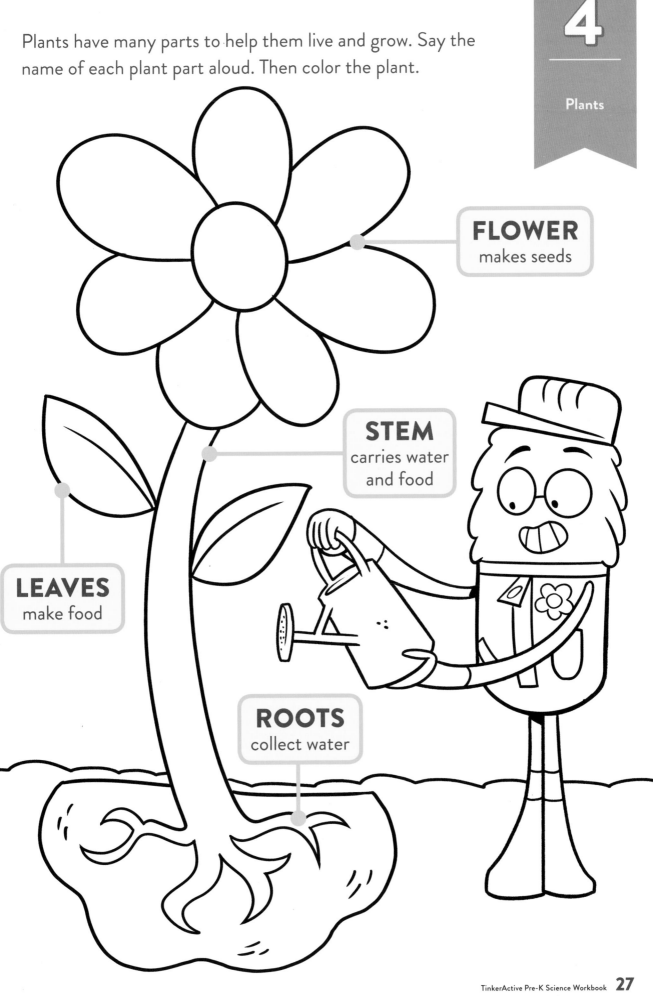

FLOWER
makes seeds

STEM
carries water and food

LEAVES
make food

ROOTS
collect water

Plants make seeds. Then new plants grow from those seeds. A new plant will look similar to the plant that the seed came from.

Look at each set of leaves. Circle the two that are from the same type of plant.

The MotMots have planted a mystery seed.

Draw the plant you think might grow from it!

Does your plant have flowers? What color are the leaves?

Different types of plants grow in different habitats. With the help of an adult, go on a plant hunt outside. Circle each type of plant you see growing in your habitat.

bush

cactus

moss

grass

fern

tree

flower

vine

Find a leaf. Hold it down with one hand, and trace it with the other. Color in your tracing to match the leaf.

Hunt for another leaf from a different type of plant! What makes the leaves different?

LET'S START!

Natural materials, like:
leaves, pine needles, sticks, seeds, flowers, bark, grass, rocks

White paper

Crayons

Paint

Rubber bands or tape

LET'S TINKER!

Use the natural materials from outside to make a model of a plant. **Show** roots to collect water. **Show** a stem to carry water and food. **Show** leaves to make food. **Show** a flower to make seeds.

LET'S MAKE: LEAF RUBBINGS!

1. Find a few leaves of different shapes and sizes.

2. Lay a leaf flat on a table. **Make** sure that the smooth top side is facing down, so that the bumpy veins on the back side are facing up.

3. Lay a sheet of paper on top.

4. Slowly **rub** over the leaf with the side of a crayon. **Watch** the leaf appear!

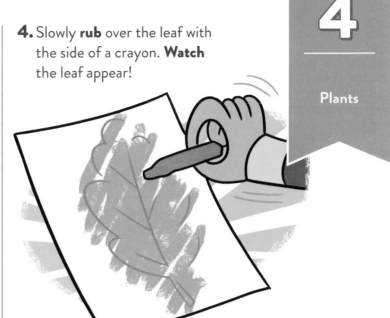

LET'S ENGINEER!

The MotMots want to paint some pictures. They have paint and paper, but they don't have any paintbrushes!

How can they use the things around them from nature to paint?

Put a stick, leaf, or piece of grass in the paint and try to paint on a piece of paper. What happens? What other materials could work? How can you combine materials to make a paintbrush? What happens when you try to use a pine needle or a rock? Or a flower? Which materials work best?

PROJECT 4: DONE!
Get your sticker!

The Earth

We live on planet Earth. It is made of many types of rock.

Draw a line to match the rocks that are the same type.
Then describe their color and texture aloud.

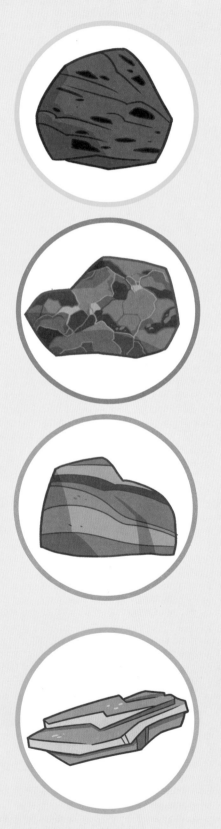
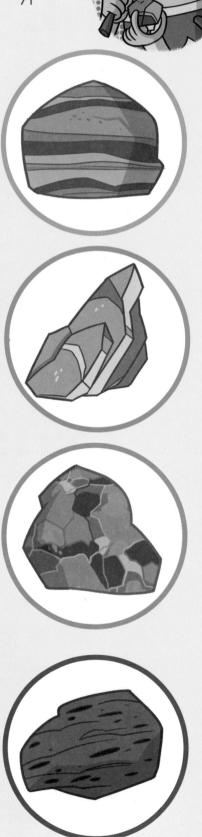

The Earth is covered in land and water. The animals and plants that live on land need air, dirt, and access to water.

Circle the living things that live on land.

Circle the living things that live in the water.

The food, water, and shelter that living things need can be found on Earth. Color the squirrel's food, water, and shelter.

With the help of an adult, read the poem aloud.

The Earth Gives Us What We Need

I live on planet Earth—
it's my favorite place to live!
Here there's water, food, and shelter.
The Earth has much to give.

The oceans give us water,
and rain falls from the sky.
We can grow crops in the fields
and eat from plants nearby!

We cut trees to make wood boards,
and build homes from what's around.
Animals can find shelter, too,
up high or underground.

The Earth gives us what we need—
I can see it's true!
There's water, food, and shelter
here for me and you.

Draw a line to match each item to the place that it comes from.

food

water

shelter

LET'S START!

6 or more rocks

Construction paper

Scissors
(with an adult's help)

Pan or large bowl

Liquid soap

Modeling clay

LET'S TINKER!

Look closely at your rocks. Can you find some that are a similar shape? What about a similar color? Or size? How many different kinds of rocks did you find?

Put them in a row from smallest to largest.

LET'S MAKE: SWIMMING FISH!

1. With the help of an adult, **cut** a small fish shape out of a piece of construction paper. It should be about as long as your finger.

2. Cut a V-shaped slot in the fish's tail.

3. Fill a pan or bowl with water about as deep as your thumb.

4. Place the fish in the water so that it floats.

5. Squirt one drop of liquid soap into the water right behind the fish, by the slot in its tail.

6. Watch it swim! You can **refill** the container with fresh water and try again.

LET'S ENGINEER!

A squirrel keeps sneaking into Amelia's house. She thinks the squirrel is looking for food, water, or shelter.

How can she show the squirrel where it can get food, water, and shelter outside her house?

Make models of the things a squirrel needs to live. Where will it get food: nuts from a tree or vegetables from someone's garden? Where will it get the water it needs: from a lake or the rain? Where will it get the shelter it needs: a hole in a tree or a burrow underground?

PROJECT 5: DONE!
Get your sticker!

The Sky

The sun, moon, stars, and clouds are in the sky. Touch the picture of each object and describe what it looks like. Then trace each name.

Go outside or look out your window. Draw a picture of what you see in the sky.

What color is the sky?

The sun is a star—a hot ball of burning gas. It rises and sets each day. During the day it gives us light and heat.

Circle the things you do during the day.

The moon can often be seen at night. Without the sun, the sky becomes darker and it is cooler outside.

Circle the things you do during the night.

Groups of stars in a pattern form a **constellation**.

Trace the line to complete the constellation of Leo the Lion.

The sun is the closest star to our planet. But at night, when the sun has set, we can often see other stars.

Start here

Clouds are made up of drops of water and ice so tiny that they float in the air. Clouds are always moving and changing.

What pictures do you see in the clouds? Draw faces to make them into animals.

Look outside. What pictures do you see in the clouds?

LET'S START! GATHER THESE TOOLS AND MATERIALS.

Paper

Newspaper

Construction paper

Paper plate

Paint
(red, orange, and yellow)

Plastic wrap

10 or more mini marshmallows

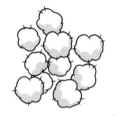
10 or more cotton balls

10 or more pieces of uncooked spaghetti

LET'S TINKER!

Use your materials to make clouds. They are always moving and changing! What shapes can you make? Do they move and change when you blow on them?

LET'S MAKE: BURNING SUN!

1. Lay your paper plate on newspaper and pour red, orange, and yellow paint on top.

2. Lay a sheet of plastic wrap on top of the plate.

3. Smoosh the paint to mix and move it around.

4. Peel off the plastic wrap and let your sun dry.

LET'S ENGINEER!

The MotMots are stargazing. They are making up their own constellations in the stars. Frank sees an alligator! He points at it to show his friends, but they can't quite tell where he's pointing.

How can Frank share the shape of his constellation with his friends?

Use your marshmallows, spaghetti, and cotton balls to design and make your own constellation to share with your friends and family! What shapes, patterns, and pictures can you make?

PROJECT 6: DONE!
Get your sticker!

Weather

The weather describes what the air outside is like. The weather is always changing.

Color the picture of weather that is rainy.

Color the picture of weather that is snowy.

Color the picture of weather that is sunny.

Color the picture of weather that is cloudy.

What do you like to do outside in each type of weather?

Circle the items that each MotMot should wear or use.

RAINY

SUNNY

SNOWY

WINDY

Observe the weather outside your window, and draw a picture of what you see.

What clothes do you need to wear to go outside? Add yourself and your clothes to the drawing.

Listen carefully. Can you hear any sounds from the weather today?

Use the stickers on page 129 to complete the snowman.

Not all places have snow! Have you ever seen snow? What do you like to do in the snow?

LET'S START! GATHER THESE TOOLS AND MATERIALS.

 10 or more cotton swabs	 Clear glass vase (or jar or cup)	 Shaving cream	 3 small bowls	Food coloring	 Small eyedropper (or ¼ teaspoon scoop)
1 cotton ball	 Piece of foil	 3–5 rubber bands	 Piece of paper	 2 or more napkins	

LET'S TINKER!

Design your own snowflake! **Start** by laying out cotton swabs on a flat surface. What patterns can you make? Is your snowflake small or big? What other materials can you use?

LET'S MAKE: COLORFUL CLOUDS!

Make these colorful clouds with the help of an adult.

1. Fill a large clear glass vase halfway with water.

2. Add a few inches of shaving cream to the top.

3. Fill three small bowls with about ¼ cup of water each. **Add** five drops of one color of food coloring to each, using a different color for each bowl.

4. Use a small eyedropper or ¼ teaspoon scoop to add a few drops of colored water to the top of the cloud.

5. Add more drops and colors, and watch what happens when it rains!

LET'S ENGINEER!

Callie was planning to take a walk outside with her dog, Boxer, but it just started raining! Callie has a rain jacket and boots she can wear. But Boxer doesn't have anything to wear to stay dry—and he hates to be wet.

How can Callie keep Boxer dry?

Pretend that your cotton ball is Boxer. **Use** your foil, rubber bands, paper, and napkins to make a covering to keep the cotton ball dry. Which materials would protect the cotton ball in the rain? How can the materials stay on the cotton ball? **Test** your idea by putting the cotton ball with its rain protection under running water in the sink. Did your design work?

PROJECT 7: DONE!
Get your sticker!

Read the poem aloud.

Four Seasons

Winter, spring, summer, fall.

Four seasons to count in all.

In the winter, bears hibernate.

But not me—I like to skate.

Spring warms up and flowers grow.

Rain falls a lot. Buds start to show.

Summer brings a break from school.

Flip-flops and shorts keep me cool.

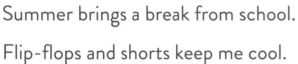

In the fall, the trees go bare.

Get ready for winter—it's in the air!

Trace the name of each season and describe the changes you see. Then circle the season it is now where you live.

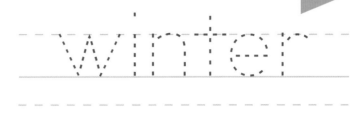

winter

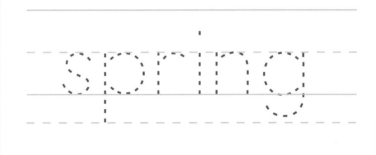

spring

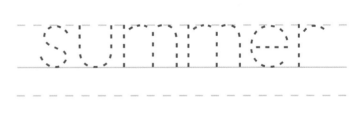

summer

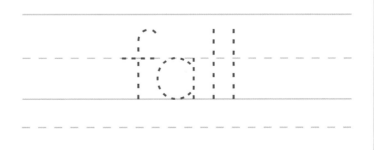

fall

Many animals respond to changes through the seasons. For example, some animals **hibernate** in the winter. This means that when the weather is cold, they go into a deep sleep. In the spring, when the weather is warmer and more food is available, they wake up.

Draw a line to lead the groundhog to its underground burrow so it can hibernate.

Many animals give birth to their babies in the spring. The weather is warm and there is more food for the mothers and babies to eat.

Draw a line to lead the skunk back to her litter of babies.

Plants respond to changes through the seasons. Point to the picture of a tree in the spring and describe what you see. Then draw a picture of what you think it will look like in the summer.

SPRING

SUMMER

People respond to changes through the seasons. Draw a line from each activity to the matching season.

spring

summer

fall

winter

LET'S START! GATHER THESE TOOLS AND MATERIALS.

Natural materials, like:
leaves, pine needles, seeds, flowers, bark, grass

Duct tape

Paper

Glue

Cotton balls

Crayons

Construction paper

LET'S TINKER!

Make a picture of a tree with your materials. Does your tree change with the seasons? If so, what would it look like in the summer?

How would it look different in the winter? What about spring and fall?

LET'S MAKE: NATURE BRACELET!

1. **Ask** an adult to help you secure a piece of duct tape inside out around your wrist. (The sticky side should be facing out—not touching your skin.)

2. Take a walk outside and watch what sticks to your bracelet!

3. Find pieces of nature that show the season and stick them on, too.

LET'S ENGINEER!

Every winter, the sheep at Tinker Town's zoo grow thicker wool to keep themselves warm. Callie also needs to dress warmly when it gets cold.

How can she keep warm in the winter?

Draw a picture of Callie on a piece of paper. Then **use** your materials to design things Callie can wear to keep warm when it is cold. What could cover her feet? Her head? Which materials would keep her warmest?

PROJECT 8: DONE!
Get your sticker!

Water & Ice

Water can be found in nature. Point to each place water is found and say the name aloud. Then trace each name.

ocean

rain

lake

river

There is also water in your home. You can use it for drinking, cooking, cleaning, and taking care of plants and animals.

Circle the places where you see water.

Hunt around your home and find three places with water.

Water is a **liquid**. Liquids have no shape—they become the shape of whatever they are in. Use a blue crayon to color each container so it looks full of water.

Juice and milk are also liquids.

Draw what you like to drink in each MotMot's glass.

When water gets very cold, it freezes and becomes ice. Ice is a **solid**. Solids are hard and have a shape.

Circle each picture that shows ice and say the name aloud.

ice cube

iceberg

rain

waterfall

icicle

When ice gets warmer, it melts and becomes water again. Draw what will happen to the MotMots' ice sculptures on a hot day.

BEFORE

AFTER

LET'S START!

Large bowl

Water

Small water-safe items, like:
a paper clip, cotton ball, pinecone, rock, leaf

Washable paint

Old ice cube tray

Spoon

Thick paper

Baking tray

Foil

LET'S TINKER!

With the help of an adult, **fill** your bowl halfway with water. Then **pick up** one small item. Do you think it will sink or float? **Make** a prediction and then drop the item into the bowl. Were you correct? **Make** predictions for all your items and then test them out!

LET'S MAKE: FROZEN SOLID PAINT CUBES!

1. With the help of an adult, **squeeze** washable paint into an ice cube tray so each cube is about half full.

2. Add water to each cube and stir with a spoon.

3. Put the tray in the freezer.

4. Place a piece of thick paper onto a baking tray.

5. When the cubes are fully frozen, **pop** them out on the paper and move them around on the paper to make a picture!

LET'S ENGINEER!

Frank and Dimitri entered Tinker Town's winter ice sculpture competition. This year's challenge is to break the mold and make interesting shapes out of ice!

How can they make ice into new shapes?

Make your own ice mold out of a piece of foil. **Try** wrapping the foil around a small toy or around your hand. What new shape can you make? Then, with the help of an adult, **fill** it with water and put it in the freezer. The next day, **take out** your ice sculpture!

ICE SCULPTURE CONTEST

PROJECT 9: DONE!
Get your sticker!

Taking Care of the Earth

People, animals, and plants live on the Earth. It's our job to take care of it! One way to keep the Earth clean is to put garbage in trash bins.

Draw a line from each piece of garbage to the trash bin.

When garbage isn't put in trash bins, it can sometimes get into the oceans.

Cross out the things that don't belong in the ocean.

Another way to take care of the Earth is to recycle. Recycling happens when something that has been used is changed into something that can be used again.

Draw a line from each piece of glass to the glass recycling bin.

Draw a line from each piece of paper to the paper recycling bin.

With the help of a family
member, find some used
paper that you can recycle!

PAPER

Another way to take care of the Earth is to fix things that are broken instead of throwing them away.

Draw a line from each broken object to the object that can fix it.

You can also take care of the Earth by reusing things instead of throwing them away. Draw a line to match each object to a way that it could be used again.

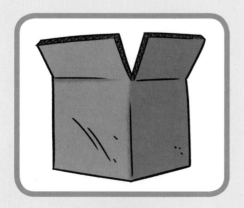

LET'S START!

GATHER THESE TOOLS AND MATERIALS.

Paper

Broken crayons

Assorted items, like:
string, a glass cup, a plastic toy

Muffin tin

Oven mitt

Scissors
(with an adult's help)

Toilet paper tube

Glue

LET'S TINKER!

Look closely at your materials. Are any of them made from recyclable materials? **Draw** four signs: one each for glass, plastic, metal, and paper. Then **sort** your materials into piles based on what they are made of.

LET'S MAKE: RECYCLED CRAYONS!

1. Peel the labels off the broken crayons.

2. In a muffin tin, **fill** a cup to the top with broken crayons. (If you have enough crayons to fill more cups, keep going!)

3. With the help of an adult, use an oven mitt to **place** your muffin tin in a 275-degree oven.

4. With the help of an adult and an oven mitt, **take** the muffin tin out of the oven once the crayons are completely melted (about 10 to 15 minutes).

5. Let the crayons cool overnight before using them. (Or cool them for 20 minutes on a cooling rack and then 10 minutes in the fridge.)

LET'S ENGINEER!

Oh no! Callie's toy robot broke. She knows that one way to take care of the Earth is to fix things that are broken instead of throwing them away.

How can she make a new head and arms to fix her robot?

Build your own robot! **Start** with a toilet paper tube. **Use** paper, scissors, glue, and other materials to add a head and arms to your robot. What other parts can you add? Does your robot have buttons, antennae, or wheels?

PROJECT 10: DONE!
Get your sticker!

You can use your senses to learn more about the world around you.
Read the poem aloud.

WHAT'S INSIDE?

I wonder what's inside this bag.

I know just what to do!

I can touch it, see it, hear it,

and smell and taste it, too.

It feels bumpy in my hand,

and it breaks apart like crumbs.

I see some little white shapes.

And I smell butter—oh YUM!

When I move the bag, I hear it shake.

It goes CRUNCH in my mouth.

It's sweet and salty on my tongue.

My five senses help me out!

Circle what is inside the bag.

You can **see** with your eyes. Eyes come in many different colors.

Look at the eyes of your family or friends. Then color in one eye on the chart for each person. Which eye color did you see the most of?

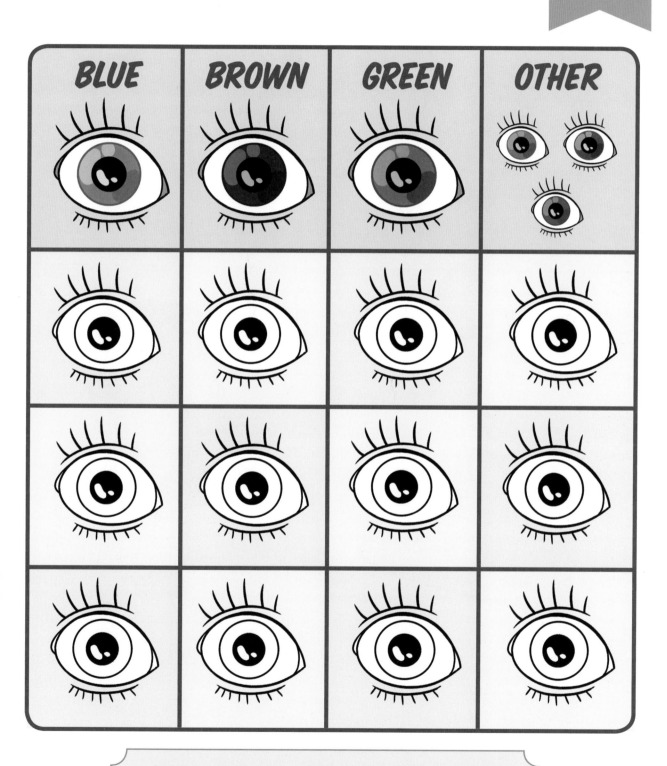

Look in the mirror. What color are your eyes? Color in an eye on the chart for yourself!

You can **hear** with your ears.

Go outside or open a window and listen. Circle the things that you just heard.

What is the loudest sound you can make? What is the softest sound you can make?

You can **touch** with your skin. Hunt for objects that match each description. Then touch and draw them.

cold

smooth

fluffy

sticky

You can **smell** with your nose.
Some things smell good and
some smell bad.

Circle the things that you
like to smell.

You can **taste** with your tongue. When food goes into your mouth, taste buds on your tongue tell you if the food tastes sweet, salty, sour, or bitter.

Draw your favorite foods on the plate. Describe aloud how they taste.

LET'S START!

Small items, like:
rocks, paper clips, cotton balls, uncooked rice

Paper bag

Liquid soap

Cornstarch

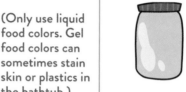

Muffin tin
(or ice cube tray)

Liquid food coloring

(Only use liquid food colors. Gel food colors can sometimes stain skin or plastics in the bathtub.)

Jar or plastic bottle with a lid

8 or more coins

LET'S TINKER!

Ask a friend or family member to place one small item into the paper bag. Without looking in, **reach** your hand into the bag. Can you guess what it is just by using your sense of touch? **Take** turns—you can place an item inside for someone else to guess!

LET'S MAKE: BATH-TIME PAINTS!

1. With the help of an adult, **add** 1 tablespoon of liquid soap and 1 teaspoon of cornstarch to each of 4 cups in a muffin tin.

2. With the help of an adult, **add** one drop of a different color of food coloring into each cup and mix the ingredients together.

3. Take the paints into the bathtub! You can **use** a paintbrush or your fingers to start painting. What do the paints look like? How do they feel on your body? Can you smell them?

4. Wash them away!

LET'S ENGINEER!

Dimitri has started a coin collection. He would like to store his coins in a jar, but every time he wants to add a coin, his cat is napping! When he tries to drop a coin into the jar, the loud sound wakes her up.

How can Dimitri place his coins into his jar quietly?

Drop your coins into your jar. What does it sound like? Can you place them in quietly? How can your other materials help? **Try** placing the rocks, uncooked rice, paper clips, or cotton balls in the jar. How do they change the sound of your coins dropping?

PROJECT 11: DONE!
Get your sticker!

Observing & Sorting Objects

There are many ways to describe and sort the objects around you.

Circle the **bigger** object.

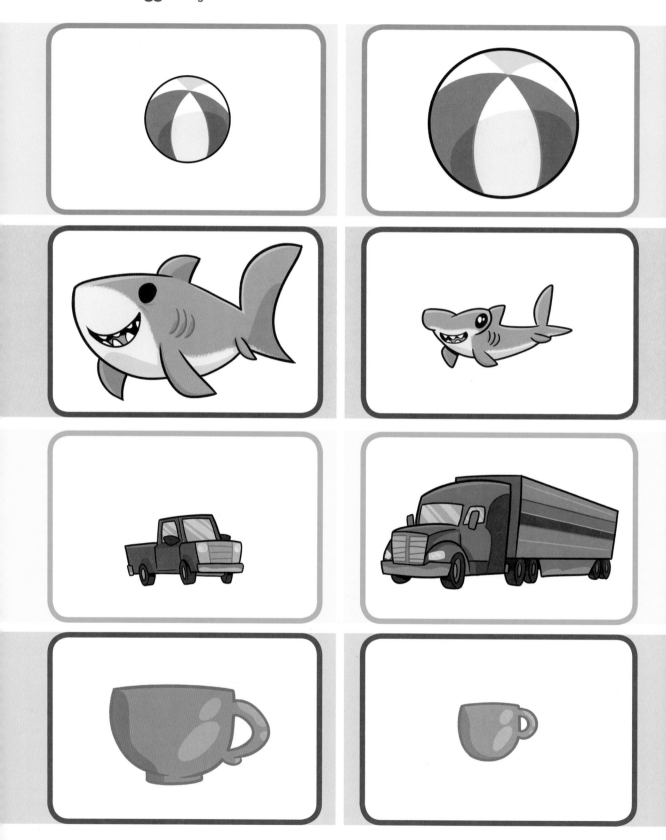

Circle the **smaller** object.

Circle the **heavier** object.

Circle the **lighter** object.

Draw lines to match objects that are the **same color**.
Say the name of each color aloud.

Observe the objects around you. Find two objects that you can pick up. Draw each object below.

Circle the object above that is **bigger**.

Cross out the object above that is **smaller**.

Find two more objects that you can pick up. Draw each object below.

Circle the object above that is **heavier**.

Cross out the object above that is **lighter**.

Find an object that is **soft** and draw it with a pencil.

Find an object that is **hard** and draw it with a pencil.

Find your favorite object and draw it with a pencil. Then circle the words that describe it.

big   small   heavy   light   hard   soft

What color is your object? Color your drawings!

LET'S START! GATHER THESE TOOLS AND MATERIALS.

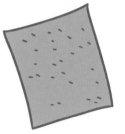
Sheet of sandpaper

Scissors
(with an adult's help)

Colored yarn
or string

Paper plate

Crayons

Glue

Assorted small and colorful items, like:
plastic bottle tops, flowers, leaves

Cotton balls

Markers

LET'S TINKER!

Lay the piece of sandpaper in front of you. With the help of an adult, cut pieces of yarn in different lengths. Lay the yarn on the sandpaper to make different shapes. Can you make shapes that are big and small? What about round or square?

LET'S MAKE: COLOR COLLAGE!

1. **Draw** three lines to divide a paper plate into six equal sections.

2. **Color** each section with crayons: red, orange, yellow, green, blue, and purple.

3. Glue materials with matching colors in each section, such as scraps of paper, yarn, plastic bottle tops, leaves, and more.

4. Look for other items around your home that you could add and glue them on!

LET'S ENGINEER!

The MotMots made a collection of critters in art class. Amelia made a critter that is big! Brian made a critter that is heavy. They'd like to take them home, but they are TOO big and heavy.

How can they make more critters that are smaller and lighter?

Use your materials, glue, and a marker to make critters that you can carry in your hand. You can also **use** the eyeball stickers on page 129. Which material could make a small critter? Which material could make a light critter? What about soft? How else would you describe them?

PROJECT 12: DONE!
Get your sticker!

Comparing Objects

To **compare**, look at how the objects are the same and how they are different.

Circle the objects that are the **same**.

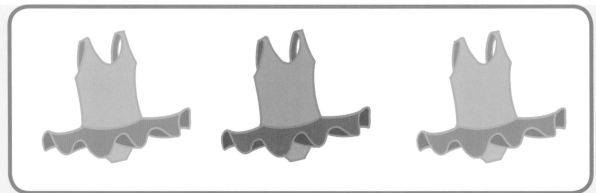

Cross out the object that is **different**.

Point to five things in the pictures that are the **same**.

Circle five things in the pictures that are **different**.

Point to five missing pieces in Frank's robot costume. Use the stickers on page 129 to make the pictures the **same**.

Draw a line to match each pair of animals that are the **same type**.

Tell a friend or a family member about your favorite animal. Then ask about their favorite animal. How are they the same or different?

Draw a shape that is the **same**.

Draw a shape that is **different**.

LET'S START!

GATHER THESE TOOLS AND MATERIALS.

10 or more paper cups

Water

Food coloring

Spoon

2 bowls

Milk

Liquid soap

LET'S TINKER!

Fill two paper cups each halfway with water. Then **use** food coloring to add a few drops of different colors to one cup and stir it with a spoon. What color did you make? **Try** to mix the same color in the second cup! Then, using fresh water, **try** to make it different.

LET'S MAKE: RAINBOW PUDDLES!

1. **Fill** two bowls each with a small amount of milk.

2. **Add** a few drops of food coloring to the middle of each bowl of milk. **See** if you can make both look the same!

3. **Squeeze** three drops of liquid soap into the middle of each bowl (on top of the colors) and watch what happens! Do they look different now?

When you are done, pour the soapy milk down the sink drain.

LET'S ENGINEER!

Tinker Town and Bungleburg were racing to see who could build the tallest tower—but both teams were rushing and both towers collapsed! So they decided to work together and build two towers that are exactly the same.

How can the engineers design and build two towers that are exactly the same?

Use your paper cups to build a tower. Then **try** to build another one that is exactly the same. How can you check that it is the same? Does it use the same number of cups? Is it the same height? Did you find any differences?

PROJECT 13: DONE!
Get your sticker!

Making Objects Move

Color the things in the picture that are moving.

Circle the object that is moving **faster** in each picture.

Pushes and pulls can make things move. Pushing moves things away from you.

Circle each MotMot who is **pushing**.

Pulling moves things toward you.

Circle each MotMot who is **pulling**.

Nonliving things can't move on their own, but you can make them move.

Find objects around your home that you can do each action with. Draw the object below that matches each movement.

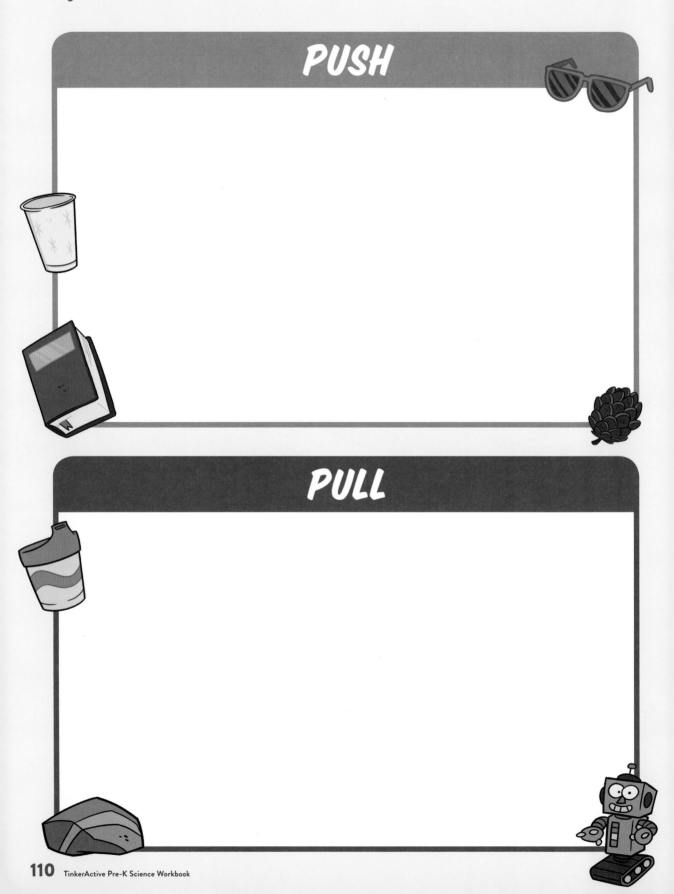

PUSH

PULL

ROLL

DROP

LET'S START! GATHER THESE TOOLS AND MATERIALS.

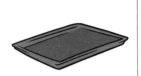
Baking tray
(or shoebox lid)

Paper

Washable
paint

Small objects, like:
a penny, dried pasta,
a pinecone, a fork

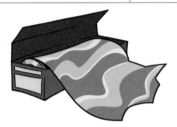
Foil

Cardboard

Rubber bands

Paper clips

LET'S TINKER!

Push and pull to move your
materials. Which move in straight
lines? Which move in zigzag lines?
Which are fast and which are slow?
Which can you roll the farthest?
Challenge a friend or family
member to a race!

LET'S MAKE: PUSH-AND-PULL PAINTING!

1. Lay a
piece of
paper
inside a
tray.

2. Pour
washable
paint into
the middle.

3. Take a small object that can get paint on it, like a penny, a piece of dried pasta, a pinecone, or a fork.

4. Push your object through the paint and watch what happens.

5. Then **pull** your object through the paint and watch what happens.

6. Add another color and try again!

LET'S ENGINEER!

Callie and Brian went to play in the snow at Thrill Hill. Callie built the bottom of a snowman at the bottom of the hill. Brian built the top of the snowman at the top of the hill.

How can they move their snowman parts to each other and finish their snowman?

Roll foil into balls to model your snowman parts. Then **use** your materials to build something to move the foil balls. How can you move the snowman parts from one place to another? Can you attach anything to the foil? Can you push or pull it? How else can you move your snowman parts?

PROJECT 14: DONE!
Get your sticker!

People can make objects change. Read the poem aloud.
Then color the picture.

I Can Change Things!

I can change things—watch me go!
Pop it. Drop it. Give it a throw.

Mix it, smash it, or shake it now.
Bend or bite it, I'll show you how.

Cut it, shut it, or use some glue.
I can change things, and you can, too!

Animals can make objects change, too.

Draw a line to match each animal to a change it has made.

Heat can make objects change.

Draw a line to match each food to a picture of what happens when it is heated up.

Cold can also make objects change.

Draw a line to match each object to a picture of what happens when it is frozen.

What changes do you feel when you go outside in the cold? Point to different parts of Enid's body and describe what you feel.

Tools can be used to make objects change.

Circle the tool that was used to change each object.

| BEFORE | AFTER | TOOLS |

You can make objects change, too.

Predict what will happen to the objects. Draw your prediction.

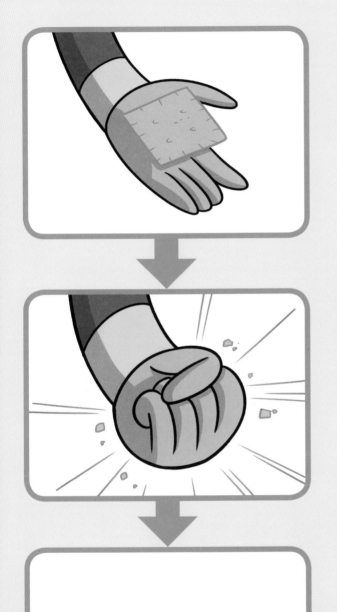

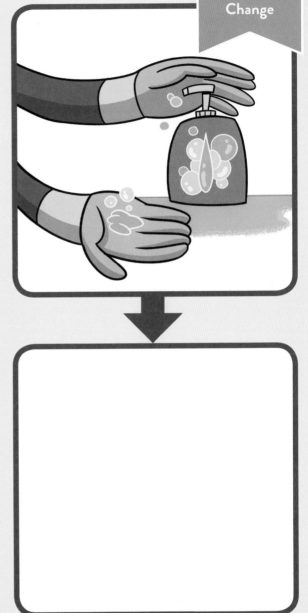

Test your prediction! Go to a
sink and put soap on your hands.
Then rub them together.
What happens? Was it what
you predicted? (Don't forget
to rinse your hands!)

LET'S START!

GATHER THESE TOOLS AND MATERIALS.

 Red, yellow, and blue paint	Paper	2 bananas	Bowl	 Fork and spoon	1½ cups quick-cooking oats	 Chocolate chips, raisins, or nuts (optional)
 Baking tray	Butter or oil	 Baking soda	Cup	 Foil	1 cup white vinegar

LET'S TINKER!

Place three small blobs of paint on a piece of paper: red, yellow, and blue. What colors can you make if you mix two of them together with your fingers? What does yellow look like when you mix it with a little bit of red? What about when you mix it with a lot of red? What happens when you mix all the colors together? **Paint** a picture with all your new colors.

LET'S MAKE: BANANA OATMEAL COOKIES!

1. Peel two bananas and place them in a bowl. **Mash** them with a fork.

2. Dump the oats into the bowl. **Add** a small handful of chocolate chips, raisins, or nuts, if you'd like.

3. Mix all the ingredients together.

4. Grease the baking tray with butter or oil.

5. Place a spoonful of the mixture on the tray and flatten it into a cookie shape. **Do** this again until all the mixture is gone. It will make about twelve cookies.

6. With the help of an adult, **bake** the cookies at 350 degrees for 15 to 17 minutes. Let them cool and then take a bite!

LET'S ENGINEER!

Dimitri loves volcanoes! He loves the hot lava! He loves how the Earth changes! And he wants to see an eruption with his very own eyes.

How can he build his own volcano?

With an adult's help, **scoop** 1 teaspoon of baking soda into a cup. **Place** it on a baking tray. Can you use foil to build the shape of a volcano around the cup?

Pour a bit of vinegar into the baking soda. What do you see? **Try** again by dumping out the cup and then adding more baking soda. What happens when you add a lot of vinegar? How can you make the biggest eruption?

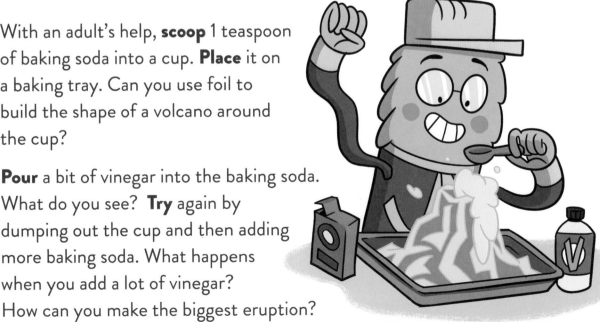

PROJECT 15: DONE!
Get your sticker!

ANSWER KEY

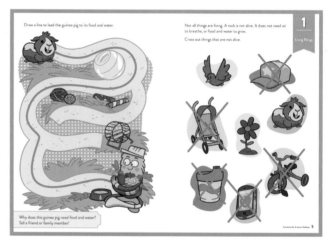

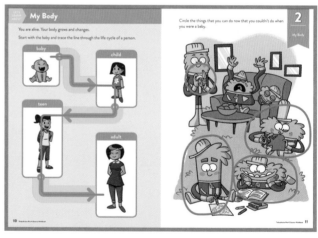

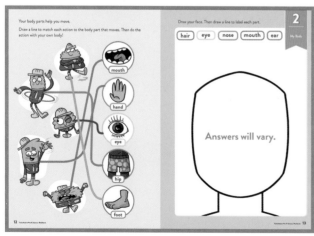

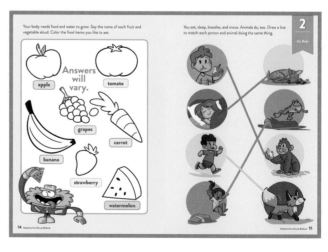

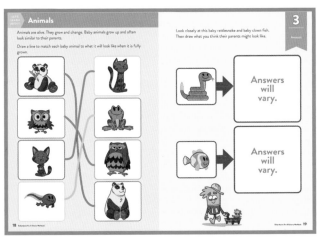

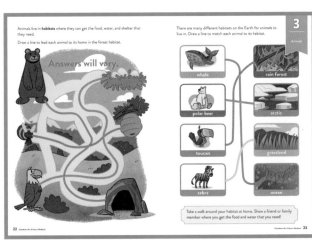
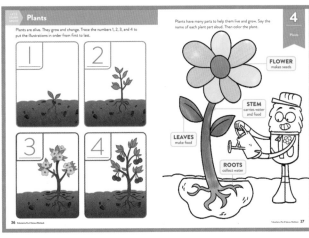

With the help of an adult, read the poem aloud.

The Earth Gives Us What We Need

I live on planet Earth—
it's my favorite place to live!
Here there's water, food, and shelter.
The Earth has much to give.

The oceans give us water,
and rain falls from the sky.
We can grow crops in the fields
and eat from plants nearby!

We cut trees to make wood boards,
and build homes from what's around.
Animals can find shelter, too,
up high or underground.

The Earth gives us what we need—
I can see it's true!
There's water, food, and shelter
here for me and you.

Draw a line to match each item to the place that it comes from.

food

water

shelter

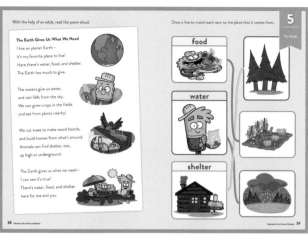

The Sky

The sun, moon, stars, and clouds are in the sky. Touch the picture of each object and describe what it looks like. Then trace each name.

clouds

sun   moon

stars

Go outside or look out your window. Draw a picture of what you see in the sky.

Answers will vary.

What color is the sky?

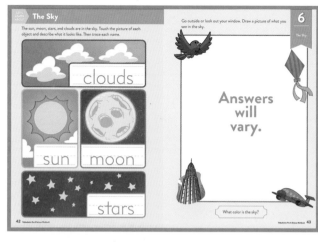

The sun is a star—a hot ball of burning gas. It rises and sets each day. During the day it gives us light and heat.

Circle the things you do during the day.

The moon can often be seen at night. Without the sun, the sky becomes darker and it is cooler outside.

Circle the things you do during the night.

Groups of stars in a pattern form a **constellation**. Trace the line to complete the constellation of Leo the Lion.

The sun is the closest star to our planet. But at night, when the sun has set, we can often see other stars.

Clouds are made up of drops of water and ice so tiny that they float in the air. Clouds are always moving and changing.

What pictures do you see in the clouds? Draw faces to make them into animals.

Answers will vary.

Look outside. What pictures do you see in the clouds?

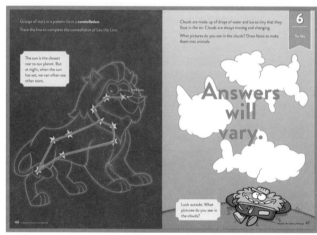

Weather

The weather describes what the air outside is like. The weather is always changing.

Color the picture of weather that is rainy.

Color the picture of weather that is snowy.

Color the picture of weather that is sunny.

Color the picture of weather that is cloudy.

What do you like to do outside in each type of weather?

Circle the items that each MotMot should wear or use.

RAINY

SNOWY

SUNNY

WINDY

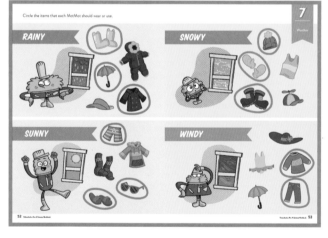

Observe the weather outside your window, and draw a picture of what you see.

What clothes do you need to wear to go outside? Add yourself and your clothes to the drawing.

Answers will vary.

Listen carefully. Can you hear any sounds from the weather today?

Use the stickers on page 129 to complete the snowman.

Answers will vary.

Not all places have snow! Have you ever seen snow? What do you like to do in the snow?

Seasons

Read the poem aloud.

Four Seasons

Winter, spring, summer, fall.
Four seasons to count in all.
In the winter, bears hibernate.
But not me—I like to skate.

Spring warms up and flowers grow.
Rain falls a lot. Buds start to show.

Summer brings a break from school.
Flip-flops and shorts keep me cool.

In the fall, the trees go bare.
Get ready for winter—it's in the air!

Trace the name of each season and describe the changes you see. Then circle the season it is now where you live.

winter

spring

summer

fall

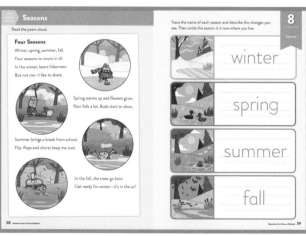

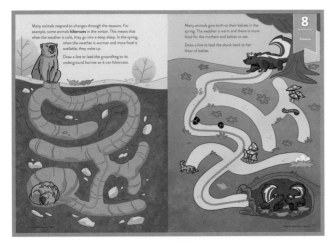

Many animals respond to changes through the seasons. For example, some animals **hibernate** in the winter. This means that when the weather is cold, they go into a deep sleep. In the spring, when the weather is warmer and more food is available, they wake up.

Draw a line to lead the groundhog to its underground burrow so it can hibernate.

Many animals give birth to their babies in the spring. The weather is warm and there is more food for the mothers and babies to eat.

Draw a line to lead the skunk back to her litter of babies.

8 — Seasons

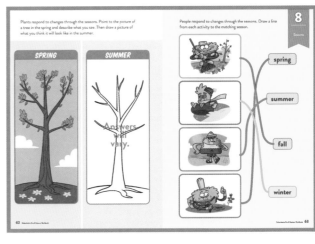

Plants respond to changes through the seasons. Point to the picture of a tree in the spring and describe what you see. Then draw a picture of what you think it will look like in the summer.

SPRING | SUMMER

Answers will vary.

People respond to changes through the seasons. Draw a line from each activity to the matching season.

spring
summer
fall
winter

8 — Seasons

Water & Ice

Water can be found in nature. Point to each place water is found and say the name aloud. Then trace each name.

ocean   rain   lake   river

There is also water in your home. You can use it for drinking, cooking, cleaning, and taking care of plants and animals.

Circle the places where you see water.

Hunt around your home and find three places with water.

9 — Water & Ice

Water is a **liquid**. Liquids have no shape—they become the shape of whatever they are in. Use a blue crayon to color each container so it looks full of water.

Juice and milk are also liquids. Draw what you like to drink in each MotMot's glass.

Answers will vary.

9 — Water & Ice

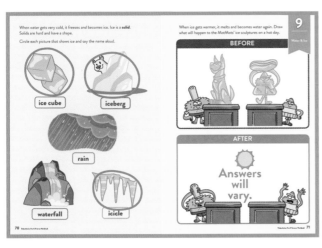

When water gets very cold, it freezes and becomes ice. Ice is a **solid**. Solids are hard and have a shape.

Circle each picture that shows ice and say the name aloud.

ice cube   iceberg   rain   waterfall   icicle

When ice gets warmer, it melts and becomes water again. Draw what will happen to the MotMots' ice sculptures on a hot day.

BEFORE
AFTER

Answers will vary.

9 — Water & Ice

Taking Care of the Earth

People, animals, and plants live on the Earth. It's our job to take care of it. One way to keep the Earth clean is to put garbage in trash bins.

Draw a line from each piece of garbage to the trash bin.

When garbage isn't put in trash bins, it can end up in the oceans. Cross out the things that don't belong in the ocean.

10 — Taking Care of the Earth

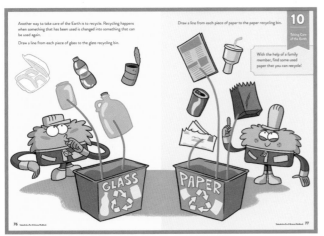

Another way to take care of the Earth is to recycle. Recycling happens when something that has been used is changed into something that can be used again.

Draw a line from each piece of glass to the glass recycling bin.

Draw a line from each piece of paper to the paper recycling bin.

GLASS   PAPER

With the help of a family member, find some used paper that you can recycle!

10 — Taking Care of the Earth

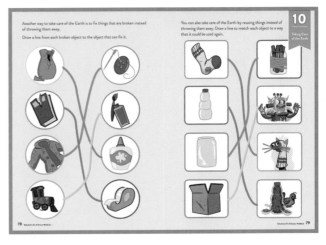

Another way to take care of the Earth is to fix things that are broken instead of throwing them away.

Draw a line from each broken object to the object that can fix it.

You can also take care of the Earth by reusing things instead of throwing them away. Draw a line to match each object to a way that it could be used again.

10 — Taking Care of the Earth

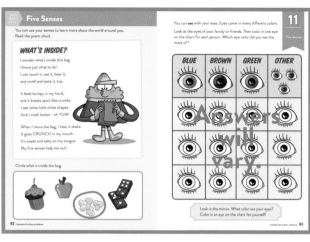

Five Senses

You can use your senses to learn more about the world around you. Read the poem aloud.

WHAT'S INSIDE?

I wonder what's inside this bag.
I know just what to do!
I can touch it, see it, hear it,
and smell and taste it, too.

It feels bumpy in my hand,
and it breaks apart like crumbs.
I see some little white shapes.
And I smell butter—oh YUM!

When I move the bag, I hear it shake.
It goes CRUNCH in my mouth.
It's sweet and salty on my tongue.
My five senses help me out!

Circle what is inside the bag.

You can **see** with your eyes. Eyes come in many different colors.

Look at the eyes of your family or friends. Then color in one eye on the chart for each person. Which eye color did you see the most of?

BLUE	BROWN	GREEN	OTHER

Answers will vary.

Look in the mirror. What color are your eyes? Color in an eye on the chart for yourself!

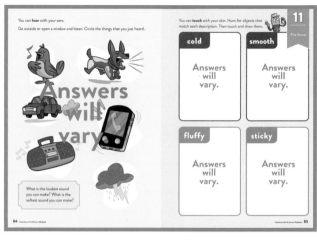

You can **hear** with your ears.

Go outside or open a window and listen. Circle the things that you just heard.

Answers will vary.

What is the loudest sound you can make? What is the softest sound you can make?

You can **touch** with your skin. Hunt for objects that match each description. Then touch and draw them.

cold — Answers will vary.

smooth — Answers will vary.

fluffy — Answers will vary.

sticky — Answers will vary.

You can **smell** with your nose. Some things smell good and some smell bad.

Circle the things that you like to smell.

You can **taste** with your tongue. When food goes into your mouth, taste buds on your tongue tell you if the food tastes sweet, salty, sour, or bitter.

Draw your favorite foods on the plate. Describe aloud how they taste.

Answers will vary.

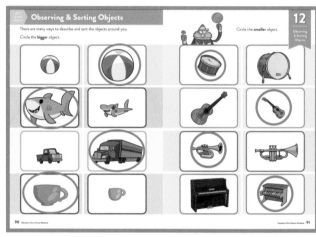

Observing & Sorting Objects

There are many ways to describe and sort the objects around you.

Circle the **bigger** object.

Circle the **smaller** object.

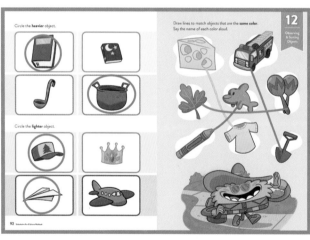

Circle the **heavier** object.

Circle the **lighter** object.

Draw lines to match objects that are the **same color**. Say the name of each color aloud.

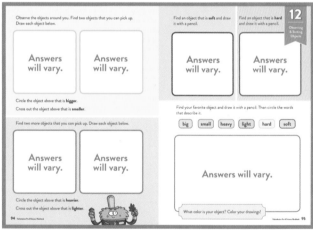

Observe the objects around you. Find two objects that you can pick up. Draw each object below.

Answers will vary. Answers will vary.

Circle the object above that is **bigger**.
Cross out the object above that is **smaller**.

Find two more objects that you can pick up. Draw each object below.

Answers will vary. Answers will vary.

Circle the object above that is **heavier**.
Cross out the object above that is **lighter**.

Find an object that is **soft** and draw it with a pencil.

Find an object that is **hard** and draw it with a pencil.

Answers will vary. Answers will vary.

Find your favorite object and draw it with a pencil. Then circle the words that describe it.

big small heavy light hard soft

Answers will vary.

What color is your object? Color your drawings!

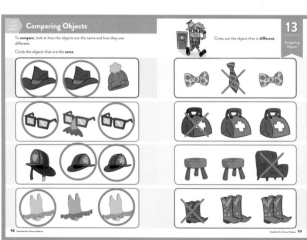

Comparing Objects

To **compare**, look at how the objects are the same and how they are different.

Circle the objects that are the **same**.

Cross out the object that is **different**.

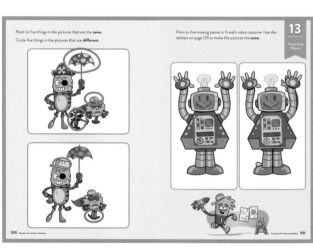

Point to five things in the pictures that are the **same**.

Circle five things in the pictures that are **different**.

Point to five missing pieces in Frank's robot costume. Use the stickers on page 129 to make the pictures the **same**.

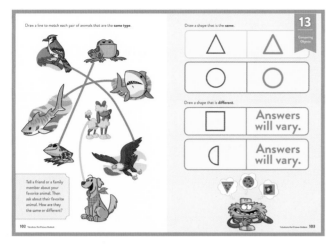

Draw a line to match each pair of animals that are the **same type**.

Draw a shape that is the **same**.

△ △

○ ○

Draw a shape that is **different**.

□ Answers will vary.

◗ Answers will vary.

Tell a friend or a family member about your favorite animal. Then ask about their favorite animal. How are they the same or different?

13 — Comparing Objects

Making Objects Move

Color the things in the picture that are moving.

Circle the object that is moving **faster** in each picture.

14 — Making Objects Move

Pushes and pulls can make things move. Pushing moves things away from you.

Circle each MotMot who is **pushing**.

Pulling moves things toward you. Circle each MotMot who is **pulling**.

14 — Making Objects Move

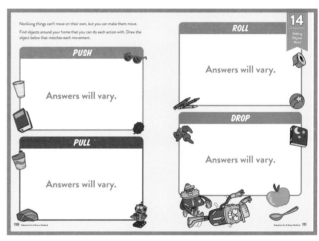

Nonliving things can't move on their own, but you can make them move.

Find objects around your home that you can do each action with. Draw the object below that matches each movement.

PUSH

Answers will vary.

PULL

Answers will vary.

ROLL

Answers will vary.

DROP

Answers will vary.

14 — Making Objects Move

Making Objects Change

People can make objects change. Read the poem aloud. Then color the picture.

I Can Change Things!

I can change things—watch me go!
Pop it. Drop it. Give it a throw.

Mix it, smash it, or shake it now.
Bend or bite it, I'll show you how.

Cut it, shut it, or use some glue.
I can change things, and you can, too!

Animals can make objects change, too.

Draw a line to match each animal to a change it has made.

15 — Making Objects Change

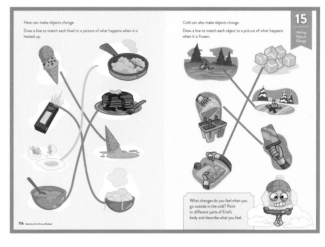

Heat can make objects change.

Draw a line to match each food to a picture of what happens when it is heated up.

Cold can also make objects change.

Draw a line to match each object to a picture of what happens when it is frozen.

What changes do you feel when you go outside in the cold? Point to different parts of Enid's body and describe what you feel.

15 — Making Objects Change

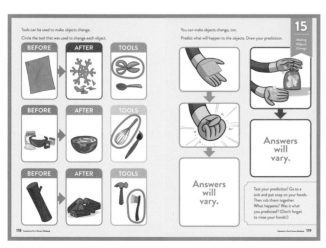

Tools can be used to make objects change.

Circle the tool that was used to change each object.

BEFORE AFTER TOOLS

BEFORE AFTER TOOLS

BEFORE AFTER TOOLS

You can make objects change, too.

Predict what will happen to the objects. Draw your prediction.

Answers will vary.

Answers will vary.

Test your prediction! Go to a sink and put soap on your hands. Then rub them together. What happens? Was it what you predicted? (Don't forget to rinse your hands!)

15 — Making Objects Change

Odd Dot
120 Broadway
New York, NY 10271
OddDot.com

ISBN: 978-1-250-20810-1

WRITER   Megan Hewes Butler

ILLUSTRATOR   Chad Thomas

EDUCATIONAL CONSULTANT   Randi House

CHARACTER DESIGNER   Anna-Maria Jung

COVER ILLUSTRATOR   Anna-Maria Jung

BACK COVER ILLUSTRATION   Chad Thomas

LEAD SERIES DESIGNER   Carolyn Bahar

INTERIOR DESIGNER   Abby Dening and Tae Won Yu

COVER DESIGNERS   Carolyn Bahar and Colleen AF Venable

EDITOR   Nathalie Le Du

Our books may be purchased in bulk for promotional, educational, or business use. Please contact your local bookseller or the Macmillan Corporate and Premium Sales Department at (800) 221-7945 ext. 5442 or by email at MacmillanSpecialMarkets@macmillan.com.

DISCLAIMER

TinkerActive is a trademark of Odd Dot.
Printed in China by Hung Hing Off-set Printing Co. Ltd., Heshan City, Guangdong Province
First edition, 2020

10 9 8 7 6 5 4 3 2 1